João

John Mateer

João

(sonnets)

Shearsman Books

Published in the United Kingdom in 2019 by
Shearsman Books
50 Westons Hill Drive
Emersons Green
BRISTOL
BS16 7DF

Shearsman Books Ltd Registered Office
30–31 St. James Place, Mangotsfield, Bristol BS16 9JB
(this address not for correspondence)

www.shearsman.com

ISBN 978-1-84861-649-3

ACKNOWLEDGEMENTS

This volume was first published in Australia, in 2018 by Giramondo Publishing, Sydney.
The author thanks its publisher and staff for their work. He would also like to thank the
editors and publishers of the following journals in which some of the poems first appeared:
Asian Literary Review (Hong Kong), *Cordite Poetry Review* and *Arc Magazine* (Melbourne/Ottawa),
Long Poem Magazine (London) and *Westerly* (Perth).

The epigraph is from Richard Zenith's translation of the poem 'Noz Numa Pedra'
by Mário Cesariny de Vasconcelos, as published on the site of Poetry International, Rotterdam.

Sure I was with Isis, but I told her my name was João.

—Mário Cesariny de Vasconcelos

Twelve Years of Travel

Merely one of the 108 Buddhist sins erased as the bell tolls,
gonging in the icy New Year night. That team
of monks stepping back, silent, from the released pole
under the TV spotlights. From in the crowd it seemed
to João the shattering of skulls numberless and holy,
pure extinction, as if all the many thousands seeing the bell,
the millions, knew by telepathy what was lurking in his soul,
that ghost. He closed his eyes, felt lost, slowly
recalling, within the depth of his dim, honeycomb body,
arriving at a temple in the far mountains of Honshu.
Pilgrims were already there, kneeling, and the monk,
blessing them with a long leafy branch, beckoned
him in to also pay homage to the transparent box,
the mummified saint. João heard: *He could also be you…*

Sublime, as the cliché would have that aria,
at breakfast in a Brisbane cafe. *Which?* João can't remember
the opera, though he does, well, the Singaporean
poet Cyril, the singer. Years later João would read, when young,
he had been an escort as well as an excellent student of voice,
confiding in the interview how he used to give sympathy
fucks to men whose lives seemed so desultory
the carnal was their only kindness. Recalling Cyril, not as castrato,
as genuine angel, João is reflecting that Sunyata, or Infinity,
is such a being, who in the midst of breakfasting poets
brings *La Traviata* and Brisvegas into a synergy
that can only be listen to unspeaking, marvelled
at. That moment was real, João feels, and worldly.
He had thought: *I hope they've noticed, too. Not just me.*

João keeps seeing in his mind that monochrome picture
of kindly Joanne, his then girlfriend, inside a dark caravel,
a real, timber caravel. She was unamused, he could tell
even then, by the surrealism of a furniture-maker in Victoria
reclaiming lumber from coastal windbreaks
to spend a decade of weekends building his ghost ship,
dreaming of sailing first to New Zealand, taking
things easy, then to on Timor, and later, of course, to Lisbon.
In contemplating Joanne's face, she seems awkward,
unhappy. Though João's remembering the comic pleasure
of that weekend: Warrnambool totally Portuguese for the festival,
Lusitania's secret celebration of discovering Australia; on the windward
side of a knoll overlooking the town their small padrão.
Maybe, in her clear, calm eyes, she had already lost her João.

João left the theatre totally appalled after hearing Rushdie
charm the audience with a sporting quip and the repartee
needed to retain the attention of fame. A million
years ago João had bought *The Satanic Verses*,
reading and reading the illicit: *This is Literature!*
But he, too, was now among them, even if still an amateur
poet in his own heart. He was staying in a downtown
hotel with Vikram, whom he'd meet again in Sri Lanka,
our João's only festival act had been talking with ghetto kids,
Afro-American, Polish, Mexican, about the Poem, its ironic
magic, while their teacher, scowling, observed him, the White
African. One of those kids asked if he knew
Swahili or Zulu. There João was again disappointing, untrue,
somehow always a ghost, slipping out of sight.

Yvonne, taller than a reed, willowy as a model,
was speaking, not kiSwahili, her gentle accent
in the Queen's English, as she led João through an ideal
museum of African art. She was saying recently
she had been to Ethiopia, loved the churches, the people,
that he should go: "They will love you: a poet, sensitive.
Besides, you are African, too." Suddenly that infinitive
was in his mind like the black bee of love-interest
buzzing in from a Mogul miniature: *To be African, able*
to move through cities knowingly... They stopped
at an Ethiopian shield of elephant hide, looking close.
Then João had an intimation of what he had been, boasting
of another life. And of a future, too;
he saw Yvonne, in Zanzibar, reciting this poem for you.

Coral arranged for them to meet at Casa del Poeta,
a dim vacancy wherein João found the usual
book-table and that intimacy of microphone and word,
everything a skull, crystal, secretive, almost invincible.
Unlike the publisher and Ruth, the elderly, bespectacled lady,
English but American, who had once translated Sophia de Mello,
really knowing only Spanish... João'd read those yellowed
pages, their Hellenic, bleached, midday hallucinations,
readying himself for his Portuguese beachcombing, Warrnambool's padrão.
Ruth was astonished he had. Then, unintentionally, he was invited
to a penthouse dinner – huge steak! – among the starry views,
Aztec antiquities. In conversation with her husband,
the Lonely Long-Distance Runner, whose novels João hadn't yet read,
he was informed they'd just arrived, from Senora, in a drug-dealer's plane.

The bliss of lime soup from the Yucatán Peninsula
tasted in an upper floor restaurant a few blocks from the Zócalo;
or an African-American, on paseo, with his tiny local wife and cigar;
or the granite snake coiled mandala-like for João's
edification in one of DF's vast museums: all are midst the squalor
of his thoughts. Very near his hotel in Zona Rosa,
on a crowded pavement, he has a déjà vu moment,
mistaking himself for Christopher Columbus in his befuddlement,
his colossal, historical – actually continental – error. João's memory
is of an identical street, but in Medan, Sumatra,
its bitter blue exhaust smoke, small talkative people,
each recognising him as the young, lost poet
João really isn't. Yet Chapultepec Park was his favourite moment,
eternally repeated, being greeted with the revolutionary: "Amigo!"

Anna said she hadn't wanted to wake you
to see the first snowflakes. This she told you
after she woke. You had been staring for hours
over the Manhattan roofs and the Hudson, out
into your long lost Canadian childhood.
She had exclaimed "João!" on arriving, exhausted,
sleepy, and you had entered one another like waves.
Last night: Anna and João on the Empire State,
alone, icy minutes before midnight. Yesterday: mistaken
for a Sugarbabe and Daddy in a West Village street,
though she was the more worldly, and you lost, near nameless.
Then: Anna laughing, sneaking into your hotel-room in Chicago,
Anna forever doing cartwheels down an autumnal avenue,
Anna, gymnast, gun-savvy, the Californian who almost loved you.

On the beach below Diamond Head the lifeguard
was confessing he hadn't used cocaine for a year.
João noted tattooed hipster chicks here
for the weekend, from Brooklyn. The usual, overheard,
reassured him Hawaii, like the rest of the US of A,
was a movie. Though this one has the Natives, before
lunch in a Filipino restaurant, singing a hymn, praying
for the bounty of Coke and pork adobo, has a dark store
in Honolulu filled with hibiscus bouquets, and, on the Big Island,
not only the small stone memorial where Captain Cook was killed
but also that empty volcanic crater, vast as God's ear,
surrounded by miles of starry black sand.
Deep in this tropical cinema João, somewhere,
swam with turtles and nymphs, followed endless, lava-strewn roads.

Naples begins with two Nigerians on a train.
João watched them. One a resident, the other visiting
with his Spanish wife. They greeted, in great detail explaining
origins, biographies. When the local was aghast, hearing
his brother had been in Rome, but hadn't seen the Vatican,
the Poet, secretly from eGoli, repressed his smile.
"You must be careful here. Napoli is worse than New York,
much worse." The local was shaking his head, likely
to enumerate crimes and suffering. Their foreboding talk
was forgotten on João's stepping from the station,
out into a bustling street lined with African stalls
leading him into an inexplicable, baroque devastation
of hot days and churches and that uncared for museum
where the statue of a goddess sprouted dog's teats.

Boatmen, stout, sweating, enjoying being crass locals
indifferent to the tourists they were rowing, paddled
in slow circles at the mouth of the Blue Grotto, complicit
with the hot sunlight, wasting time. To João, this fiddle,
as a Joburger would have called it, was defeating his hope
on coming to Capri – his only reason for visiting this boutique
of an island, to revisit this cave. Shouting, the rowers
were saying they can't enter unless they wait, though the heat
will kill the tourists… The Grotto, luminous, turquoise in João's mind,
was where his father, who couldn't swim, hesitating, trembled,
having to leap from one boat to another, before again
day would blind them with the obvious. His father, straining
in that moment, and João, a swimmer, six years old, was wanting
to hold him, wanting his dear Dad to be forever unafraid.

That was the only time in his life he'd
found someone like her, totally uninhibited.
She had kissed him immediately in that Slovene village,
in Ljubljana taken him into her narrow, student's bed.
She who was so proud of her breasts she said,
when he marvelled, "Yes, I know!" and grinned.
Together in bed they'd had to speak German.
And when they couldn't use a condom
she told him she preferred taking the risk,
and he had then sensed, happily, another future in this.
Just as when, on their last night, he had felt another past.
In bed, half-awake after fucking, she asked
what he knew of the Balkan Wars: "Near my village
there was one of those camps…" That was all she said.

Josef met João there outside Karlskirche,
at the wintermarkt, and they drank glühwein,
that resin like pantomime blood. Josef was jokey,
talking about his son, who in the time
after the Tsunami had sunk into depression, now
was better. "With his new flatmate, João,
I should say 'landlady', an old, famous punk-rocker,
he might learn more about life!" As the two of them wandered
through the stalls, the night and the noise and snow
surrounded João like a vast, dense mink coat,
like the one his mother wore in Canada, had been happy in.
Days later João would be drugged by a Galician's love-magic,
outside Stephansdom, learning from her and her wildness.
That night there were no women, though, just João and the novelist.

Long leather coat, cropped hair blond, peroxided,
the professor was in her national costume, nothing less
than what João, being a poet of strangeness, expected
from an Austrian specialist in the literature he'd come
to Europe to avoid. They sped along the autobahn,
then up a mountain for a beer-and-strudel breakfast,
downed with schnapps, before his lecture on Australian
literature – that exotic – and the Ur-Real, the Aboriginal.
Both he had to discuss: the Embassy had paid.
But when he began explaining his doubts, the nightmare
of all this, the professor agreed, saying: "I feel that there
are the Australians, 'The Whites' I mean,
who wish they could simply disappear. Then, it will also seem
to the Aborigines that the past two centuries were a terrible dream."

João arrived at the dinner and listened to the waitress
who expected fluent French, to the Australian academic
blaming people like him. There was nothing João could redress.
Anyway, he was too shaken by that sinister aspect
of the European soul he'd just, in a lane, witnessed:
Africans, his brothers, ordered out of the bars and restaurants,
lined up against the wall, having their pockets emptied,
been asked for papers. "Here, in Paris, Apartheid
is still alive," João declared. The academic and her talk
continued there in the light while the poet, in his cave, his mind,
relived the shadow-play of last night being in Chateau Rouge,
he the only non-Senegalese, and of the one man, a huge
Rastafarian taxi-driver, greeting him, extending his hand.
João, left the dinner, yearning for Africa, unconfused.

On the same day Jesper met with João – the week
of his appointment to the Swedish Academy – he had, for hours,
been interviewed by journalists. The two poets luncheoned
at a cafe opposite the Paris Opera. Jesper then took João
on a tour through the mind of a poem he, a classicist, had written,
tracing the path of Apollinaire's 'The Flute-Player.'
In Jesper's words: "Here there was a parking-lot and garbage.
Down there a pension, where a friend lived. It was a bordello."
And they entered a dim church, exited through another door,
Jesper explaining that Apollinaire, in the poem,
was reenacting the tale of the Piper of Hamelin: "Those
women who were following our Flautist were probably whores."
Pause. "That's what the poem implies," said Jesper, perturbed.
While João, the Foreigner, worried they may have been overheard.

More than Chartres Cathedral there were the town's
back-streets, stone bridges, gardens efflorescent.
If he could have said anything French our João
would have prayed to the blessed, leafy limelight sent
down from whatever's beyond the soul. Did he really sleep
out there in the willow's shade? Or was that in Portugal,
beside the Douro? He definitely had napped, dreamed deeply,
on a bench along the Champs-Élysées, and in Rodin's Garden,
though neither had this presence of verdure, the Heavenly.
The Cathedral, too, was atavistic, an elongated, petrified forest,
if with the levity of rosy stained-glass windows and a darkness
like bodiless anger. In there the pilgrims were walking slowly,
their feet sensing an intricate, inlaid maze.
Watching them on that mandala, João was silently, joyously amazed.

Kazuko was reminiscing about Iowa City and Mazisi,
the Zulu poet João admired. There was an ease
in their conversation, in the swish Tokyo hotel
where they were staying for yet another obscure festival.
In the lobby a real pianist and, in kimono, a party,
a wedding. When he asked Kazuko to autograph his book,
the Grand Lady of Surrealism wrote boldly, quickly,
ending with a large balloon heart and a flirty look
João well recognized. *Something about me*, he thought,
gives everyone hope! And upstairs, he recalled,
Coetzee once stayed here, too. The academic
João'd had a soba lunch with described the South African's novels
as science-fiction. Indeed, that common gimmick,
time-travel, is in hotels, fame and the various loves.

They dropped João outside a typical saloon bar
for him to find working there the young Brazilian girl,
the student who'd offered him a bed. As always, João
was thoroughly charmed, even with knowing he must wait till
she finished work. A drinker started explaining the quiet smile
of a sweet Dominican woman who, silent, swirled
the purple cherry, dreamily, in her drink while
listening to the story of her life. To João this all seemed
made-up, a movie, like the whole country. There were those moments,
of course, when everything was also a vivid baroque dream
à la Raúl Ruiz: that student and her curly-haired boyfriend,
both describing, with youthful languor and hope, their Brazil,
driving down to Manhattan to visit family and dance.
Fatherly, João smiled, murmured his blessing, wished them well.

What, João, were you doing there
in the three-storey brownstone mansion, uptown,
with those foreign poets, translators and the millionaire's
wife who makes TV documentaries, working now
on one about an African village where girls are fattened
for marriage? This could have saddened
you: again the half-hearted invitation, not belonging
as always… You, momentarily, thought of telling
Yvonne, your Kenyan friend, about this, their Africa,
when you remembered wandering with her
through that museum filled with spears, shields and beads.
She had been telling you: "João, you need
to come back to Africa." That night you are leaving
with some Slavic poets who are beckoning: "Hey, Mr Slovenia!"

Meet her under the tail of the dark horseman
of Wenceslas Square. The Czech translator, another Tanja,
was there to give João a tour. When at the airport meeting him
she'd said he was lucky arriving at 5 am because under
that dawn sky he would see something rare: the parade of statues
along Charles Bridge, without tourists. Now, on a whim,
she took him to see, in an arcade, an equestrian
statue inverted, horse and rider as if hung from a balloon,
the surrealism of the True. While they walked he tried
to explain what he'd confessed at the festival in Olomouc, that his Russian
was Afrikaans, a state language only forcefully legitimised.
Midway, after giving directions to some lost tourists,
Tanja was shaking her head: "I have only now realized
those Russians will think I on purpose gave wrong directions!"

No, not the sun burning over a rocky desert,
it's João, alive to this Rubenesque Czech girl, his heart.
Their hands ask them to leave the restaurant
and their kisses make the night cosy not snowy,
though nothing alters the hotel's Communist Era dankness,
that bed almost too small for pleasure. Knowing
her boyfriend is at home with flu, she tells João
not to worry, but he surprises himself, being appalled, unable
to kiss her deeper, unable to forget how culpable
he would be – the Foreigner! – and so has to walk her out. In Prague,
months later, he will try again, try roguishly,
inviting her to an exhibition of *The Devil's Bible*,
the World's Largest Book. She will laugh, a bit harshly,
and, of course, act as if she would never have been available.

It's hard to believe that when in San Francisco
he left his dear Anna curled up in bed
in that cheap Chinatown hotel when he'd gone
to luncheon with yet another famous poet. In João's head
his sweet Californian girl was always asleep,
tiny, with the aching muscles of an ex-gymnast,
her face, pale, like a Mexican Madonna's, almost weeping,
always asleep, even in her sleeping-bag during the bombast
of the Iowa tornado, safe in the womb of a basement.
Maybe João couldn't remember Anna awake
because he was afraid of recalling that day they'd raced
to her sister who, bald-headed and bankrupt, recently diagnosed
with cancer, was sitting in her hospital room surrounded with photos.
Could that be the loss he needs to unremember? Who knows?

When João looked up there was a teddy-bear
in his face and the translator behind told him
to say hello. He understood this wasn't a whim.
He spoke with her through the animism, didn't stare
at her afterwards, respecting this pet, this surrogate
baby. Though he did wonder what pain, unforgotten,
was there, carried around by his friend like a precious doll,
a suitcase of doubt. João, a year later, nearly forty,
would know enough to not ask and do as he was told,
ordering a slice of Sachertorte, at Vienna's famous Demel,
for that teddy-bear. It's mother, an extraordinary translator
of Swedish, connoisseur of Etruscan art, had also taken
him to Brooklyn Heights to view where the Twin Towers
has stood. He had wanted her to say more than: "Just look."

That history painting, he could almost not remember,
even though Per's pointing out the small scene is still clear.
They were at a party in the Governor's Palace, central Stockholm,
and João was sick from the autumnal chill. A blur
those dim days: an TV actress reciting his poems, Tranströmer
in the audience, twice falling into bed with a tall girl
who detailed the confusions of love with a married man,
and there was that exhibition of photographs by Araki.
And there would be, years hence, that meeting with Sonnevi,
in the city's Mediterranean Museum – midst
cabinets of watching stone figurines – out of the snow and mist.
They would converse for an entire afternoon, on poetry, the brain,
stuttering and jazz. To João this city was simply memory,
a house burning in his heart, that dark fame.

Probably João shouldn't have gone home
with this Kristina. There had been another girl,
equally Swedish, who'd hugged him. Not as tall
or blond or proudly confident. They weren't stoned,
nor in a sauna. João and this almost-model, both ill
with colds, fell in bed together, confessed
small crimes, embarrassments, loves. She recounted, too fully,
being kissed by an African-American in a New York hostel,
just kissed and held in his huge arms, confused
in her unanticipated orgasming. Poor João, never African enough
for these Europeans! He decided that he should be without
a love-interest now. So the next time he returned
to Stockholm he would do nothing other than meet
Göran for an afternoon at the Mediterranean Museum.

Then there are those places you drift through, like
the cemetery Per says was in *The Naked Lunch*,
like Teatr Weimar where you would, one evening,
present yourself to new strangers. Your life, not a ghosting,
João, is a passing through this world into deeper memory,
a searching for what's beyond elsewhere, an enquiry
into your previous lives. *You are the evening wind
on an African lake, that silver rippling...* You hear this friend
speaking of his sweetheart, saying that when she told him
her thesis was on poems of the Swedish North, their silence,
he had thought: *She's the one!* João, you are what they call breath,
panting inside the wind, struggling to keep up
with the inevitable march of winter, the years. *Wake up,
sleepy João! In this drifting there is no death!*

Maybe João didn't want to be like El Hombre,
the Chilean, a womanizer, an indigene. Together
they walked Copenhagen, ending up in a bar.
El Hombre was reminiscing about his first exile years,
all the blonds, the fucking, once escaping an irate boyfriend
by climbing out the window, grabbing the first midnight
taxi only to hear, as he was driven down to the waterfront,
a Finnish tango. *Like a fado, yet not*, João thought,
probably saying a word or two. Though his friend
would definitely not have heard, his presence arousing,
somehow, to a pair of twenty-year-olds there wanting
the Big City experience. Like his wife, a Danish country girl,
whom he kept talking about divorcing, even as all
their attention returned to the marble sphinx seen earlier in an empty hall.

Tomaž also kissed her hand. João hadn't seen
anything like that before. Bogdan, his Romanian friend,
had already done the same. She had slept with João,
and other poets. Once they even borrowed Bogdan's apartment!
Still, when he'd asked what she thought of that
gentlemanly act, João felt as if from Nowhere,
a barbarian from the South, a ghost from eGoli.
Communism didn't ruin them, he thought.
Whereas me, my life, is less than an open book,
really a poorly finished poem… When he saw Tomaž
greeting the Romanian, first in Slovene, then he took
a step forward and spoke that Latin tongue, not missing
a beat, as they say of those who know the heart,
João knew that to be a poet here he'd also have to play the part.

Whether this invitation had began with the essay
or that chance meeting with Tomaž, João couldn't say.
He did remember the American's essay as he lay
there across the chairs in the empty hall,
its description of this, the Slovene Writers Union, all
the ironies of Socialism, how powerful writers today
are fading like old paperbacks. There was João's pleasure, deep,
as he napped exhausted after the train journey,
dreamily recalling another season, the willowy translator, sweet,
raven-haired, he'd slept with, for the first time unselfconsciously.
This evening she would hug him on arrival in front of everyone,
embarrassing them, or him. Now that he was here, under
the watchful eye of dream, he was recalling what, years ago, she'd said:
"A man must write a book, plant a tree, father a child."

Laura arrived with her entourage of a retired art-restorer,
a British journalist, their common friend Nico. More arrived later;
that weird trio who'd spent the afternoon making a porno,
the fellow – a poet! – dizzy as a star. "What's he saying now?"
João asked his love. "He wants Laura to be in the film.
She just said, maybe she would, as long as it wasn't with him!"
That was the start of another, long Madrid night. His beloved
knew João had something for Laura, unrequited,
a kiss he'd wanted to give her when they'd been in New York moonlight.
Laura always says, "Men take marriage too seriously!" She was married,
after an early pregnancy, to an older man, kind, quiet,
not a poet. João's beloved, not apparently jealous, knew this,
yet still translated, holding him conspicuously close, later, declaring,
"Come on, João, I know what kind of film is playing in your head!"

At dinner João's friend Hector, the Catalan nationalist,
kept mistaking this girlfriend for another on the list
of exs. First, he thought she was the Australian psychologist,
then the Californian, the poet and gymnast. He kept insisting
she spoke very good Castilian, though they kept telling him
it was her language, among the five others. He was
impressed, Hector who used to confuse German and English,
who when he was at dinner with the poet the year before
had spoken Korean with his wife, Castilian with their Korean guest
and Catalan, every so often, with João by mistake,
saying, "It is like Portuguese, no?" João, always taken
by the European generosity of those who switch languages
to include the listener, thought of his Galician love's godchild,
swearing whichever tongue the boy spoke would be his, too, if in a while.

João was asked if he wouldn't mind another
passenger on the trip up to Colombo. It was the famous
Vikram João had encountered two nights before, wandering
Galle's back streets, also trying to find the party housed
in one of those renovated, walled-in palaces numberless
in the Third World. João had stayed on a bit,
watched the novelist on a chaise longue holding forth
Oxford-style, but then had left for another talk
nearby in a lane where a film strangely forecasting
the massacring of the Tamil Tigers was secretly shown.
Most of the audience locals. Vikram, leaving with them
in the van, is explaining that he had nearly been arrested by soldiers
who accused him of being a spy, out before dawn,
sitting with crows on the walls of the old fort, making sketches.

From the pool of the Galle Face Hotel
João is watching the eloquent, imperious Dalrymple
surveying the view from the balcony of his luxury room.
They had both been at the festival, south in Galle,
were now in Colombo, having already had time to roam
the island during the ceasefire, before the plane
that will crash into the city, after suicide-bombings, shame
and massacre. João hadn't planned to stay here
in this colonial hotel, enjoying sunsets, G-and-Ts
and the theatre of the long-bearded doorman, waiters
in their white coats. There, watchful, above the balcony,
soldiers at their anti-aircraft guns. Melancholy
with lost friendship, João is musing on his friend, her cancer,
how they couldn't meet due to roadblocks and the elusive husband.

All João remembers is suddenly being out
of the cave, up there on the bare rocky
terrace. The plain below was hot haze. Shouts,
and the scream of a woman, entranced,
in a worn sari, long hair matted, falling to her knees,
shuddering. Had João really just seen Portuguese soldiers
painted inside the cave, up on the ceiling over Buddhas
calm as ferns and real as this Dravidian woman,
wide eyes whitened by whatever was her possession,
frightening them with her own lost person, echoes
across blue day? Watching this distant, dusty woman
chanting in tongues unknown, inhuman: she's a cut snake
whose anger is singularly defensive, her mouth
that exited cave of petroglyphs, depths no-one can fake.

The Mouth of Hell, or Heaven? The opened doors
of the inner sanctum of the Buddha's Tooth Temple,
reminded João of his youth, of seeing gold, molten,
blinding, poured out as a sign of the origin of eGoli's ill,
its greedy, industrial existence. Like in Colombo,
when on the full-moon a week before he had stood in a temple
hearing the bare-chested keepers trumpeting on
in a raga, distant crowds abuzz, whispering their Sinhala,
here, between the people praying, João, was gone,
lost in the glow of the small golden stupa housing the Tooth.
You know, he wanted to tell someone, anyone,
early on, before the Anglophones, my Portuguese, it's true,
stole the Buddha's Tooth, publicly ground it down to a powder.
But the real Tooth had been hidden, kept its power.

In the bookshop there was the smell of greed,
more than the usual for Chaoyang, the old district
where embassies lurk in the crazy-bad smog
only to disappear behind blocks of concrete apartments
built day and night in the rush to efface every city-god.
That, and the sweat and excitement of this sadly familiar breed,
all Westerners, handmaidens to capital and its speed,
are marginally worse, he thought, *than those Embassy officials*
who'd spoken solely Mandarin at the presentation
of a curiously timely history, telling how the Chinese in the goldfields,
had been Aussies – of a kind – even before Federation.
Afterwards, the wife of its deceased author, quietly told João,
"We need more poets." Indeed, as at this book launch now.
When China Rules the World. Yes – a book, and an abomination!

This small terracotta army prepared for fighting ghosts,
or whatever's in the Afterlife, is unvisited by tourists.
João only came here to behold their miniaturisation that hosts
memory and dream. These figures and their shadows the insisting
that we humans don't live in our skulls, not even in China,
not even outside Xian, with its empty freeways, property mania,
skies so polluted they're only cleared by exploding rockets.
We know João, our poet, loves museums, objects and their fame.
Sometimes, in lucid dream, he is a god storming through forests
of gigantic lotuses and skeletal trees bearing – not fruit – jewels,
to come upon a glade of crows or a lonely beach…
Remembering the clay warriors, the horsemen and commanders, each
dedicated to the habit of war, that human selfishness,
João tells himself: "Become Nothingness, that golden wilderness!"

On another day in Macau the poet was nearing A-Ma Temple.
Actually he was stopped outside a Macanese restaurant,
was contemplating the menu, wondering if he had ample
time for lunch. *One of the approaching passers-by can't
be Weinberger of Manhattan…?* There'd been a poetry festival
in Hong Kong. Indeed, beside him: *Gary Snyder, Bei Dao!*
They were going for lunch. Would João like to
join them? He can't remember the food, but João
has, verbatim, some of the poets' conversation.
Unfortunately, clearest when Snyder asked if he was Australian
and he answered, "Do you want my passport?"
Mistakenly and terribly brusque. João regretted that.
Yet Snyder afterwards, outside the restaurant, in the talk
of farewell, smiling: "Real great to meet you here, on the Macau sidewalk!"

The two Americans were debating Civilization,
whether, as Weinberger had proposed, there ever was a great
era for poetry without the era also being sensational
for those angels, as João'd once nominated translators,
those close-listeners. Snyder was proposing one counter-example
after another, and Eliot, his long-time friend, true New Yorker,
was dismissing each. Bei Dao, seemingly of even fewer
words than his rare poems, had, maybe,
in mind what he would later say: that Macau,
always a haven from Greater China, free,
was still an island of gamblers, prostitutes, poets, Portuguese,
for those who no longer know how to go home… How
could he, exiled, justify his new, Hong Kong life, teaching bored,
spoilt students who don't even read? This he would confess to João.

There are those old colonial cities peopled as if by ghosts,
smugglers and poets, where chance meetings
can lead to friendships, initiate chronicles, where hostesses
in karaoke bars, possibly in silk brocade dresses,
pull aside curtains to reveal, in a black suit,
Carlos, who is immediately talking about Indian saints,
Pessanha and reading Burton's *1001 Nights.*
Or where his friend, Anabela, insists João
visit the Venetian Casino, "Because this is Macau!"
in the Thai restaurant where, at the end of their night,
the Pinoy ladyboys go to sing and drink. Loud,
festive, differently haunted, that restaurant's
scene reminds João of how little he really knows
about the world. In that crowd, his innocence shows.

Last time João was in Singapore Abdul had taken
him to the Keramat of Radin Mas, the princess,
where Abdul'd explained how his aunt, who'd been seeing
evil visions, was exorcised on the dukun's advice,
having his sister remarry, correctly, in Javanese dress,
to not anger the ancestral spirits. "Now I'm more stressed,"
Abdul is saying. "Not long ago my family
discovered my father has, for twenty years,
another wife and a family, that he has been secretly
supporting. So now I am afraid
they want half of my father's pension." João's good friend,
once his student, was here teaching him about real ghosts,
the unforgotten, the eternal responsibility of the son. "Worse,"
Abdul says, "Even at his age he is still obsessed with sex!"

Were João to – beyond his recollection – film
what took place on the bridge between worlds, in Istanbul,
where he found Marjan, the Slovene, loping along,
the Islamic city a hazy, dull blue, and they were almost alone,
poets on the Thieves Bridge, he would have that monochrome scene
silent, and his friend's look on seeing him would then seem
astonished, if slowly, as if João were one of the Christian
dead, one of the arizen, coming through the insistent mist,
from a past that could be focused. Anyone watching them
would hallucinate subtitles, in Aramaic or Ancient Armenian,
and the outward sweep of the deep mandala of meeting and friendship.
Out of sight, standing arms crossed, would be João's beloved,
as always annoyed by the mistreatment of poets,
feigning annoyance at this meeting, its faux-silence.

João remembered that Mediterranean, night,
its obsidian mirror flicking the specks of shiplights
into his skull hollower and larger than the West.
What are we, he wondered, *we, two of the Lost,*
still believing in Literature and Thought, the madness
of our absent fathers? He a poet and she a polyglot air-hostess,
one of those angels pacing the catwalks of the clouds,
reassuring passengers they won't free-fall... At reception, allowed
a room away from the pilots and the always gay crew,
they hoped to undress, fuck, video themselves, not argue.
But there João was on the balcony, contemplating the dark.
Tomorrow the Parthenon's gates will not be unlocked,
and one of her colleagues will find them in a park,
mid-argument. João, sadly, will remember a statue's lifted foot, that art.

In Leipzig João didn't see the vast stone monument
to the German army who battled mad Napoleon.
Instead, on this grey afternoon, there was that moment
when at the Institute Josef showed him, as if from a podium,
the view from his large, bright office window
and quipped: "The bad side is that you don't know
if they will bomb that building there – the American
Consulate." João looked and saw, not pandemonium,
only distant autumn leaves, burning and tumbling.
When, just before his reading, in the dark evening,
João had tried to reflect on his day at the Leipzig Book Fair,
on his afternoon with the novelist, most clearly
he remembered Josef saying he often taught in a morgue,
kept Marx's *Collected Works* in the library as a memento mori.

Kurdish, born in the East, Sherko, now a German novelist,
took João and his Galician girlfriend on a little wander
through disappeared Berlin, past statuesque Russian hookers
in high boots and fur coats, briefly, comically insisting
that the girls'd had that corner since before the Fall
of the Wall. And they walked along streets, following
the dotted line that for decades had divided the world.
Sherko stopped at a doorway, on the threshold,
pointed out a small plaque. "There are many across the city,
placed here to commemorate the Jewish fatalities."
He wouldn't speak about his Kurdistan novels. Nor did João
say anything about nearly weeping at Checkpoint Charlie,
seeing the ersatz soldier stamping, comically, any passport,
as if nations, wars and flight were merely random projects.

João didn't tell his girlfriend that in the basement
of Schloss-Leopoldskron a whole Nazi family suicided;
in the ballroom they had filmed *The Sound of Music.*
In one of its many bedrooms he and his muse slept
in a bed wide as landscape. All so he could read African
poems to a student audience in the baroque light
of mirrors tarnished with quiet. One of the translators,
maybe a rightist, was João's German voice and that man's
wife-to-be a muted smile. João thanked Shakyamuni
his Galician love was here to witness all this, the better side
of the Mitteleuropean character. That city of Mozart's birth,
according to dear Thomas Bernard, is the worst place on Earth.
Though to João and his beloved on that one night evil
couldn't exist: a full moon held the palace and lake still.

Know this: a BDSM dungeon is a theatre, carnally
internal, especially in Melbourne. Not that, really,
João and his beloved were ever there. Not that her lily-bright flesh
marks up easily, bruises photogenic. João seriously
didn't know who he was, where that dominant he then was
had been before. So there he was, asking her indifferently,
she on one leg, teetering, hands tied, to do her best:
"Don't fall over." Another push, lightly, politely, causing
her anger, tears and that wonderful shuddering tight as a fist
around her heart. Neither of them were cursing
anyone, nor God. Then she was lying on the leather bench
in the whirling room that knows no bounds, rehearsing
the birth of their child, or João's admission into a monastery,
of course, Buddhist. For her, the Catholic, this was enough mystery.

The postcard showed a becak driver asleep
wearing a Superman T-shirt. João could tell
his old becak driver saw the joke truly, and well
understood. Beyond his own poor bahasa, from deep
in his heart João meant this: *Pak, you may be 72*
with legs like pistons and a wrinkled, mountainous face,
yet midst all kinds of humble professionals you
are a bodhisattva to those who can see them in places
like this, this Yogya of exhaust fumes and fast desolation…
João understood the old man's superhuman simplicity,
something the Indonesian could teach him. But, in a confusion,
João had watched this old becak driver, his near complicity,
not being shocked, on witnessing an accident, one man
knocked down in the street; how he'd just peddled past, deadpan.

Vomiting as critique, João thought bent
over in the millionaire's dark Balinese garden,
while in the marquee the other writers went
through the motions of being gracious. Forgotten
was introspection; they were just acting true
to their personae. Then he wiped his face,
went back to the table where he and others, too,
watched those more famous. "My disgrace,"
he quipped, "is that affluence makes me sick!"
His mind loved the tropical opulence, his body,
though, was still political. No laughter. Restricting
himself to French, the Egyptian writer, now less moody,
was again bragging to a younger Australian woman.
João, like the watching servants, was alone, forgotten.

"Lost Boy and Mother Africa" is how he described them,
himself and yet another novelist, roaming post-revolutionary Cairo.
Rezinat, a proud woman, a fashion queen, true Nigerian,
who ate with her hands, calling for chilli, always saying, "You know,
in my country, Nigeria," detailing its superiority. Excepting the pyramids,
she was unimpressed, Egypt just a country of Arab men
wanting to chat her up, and of nearly First World medicine.
Once, at dinner, looking around, shaking her head,
shifting her headscarf back: "I mean, look at this place!
But they have electricity, power and lights, without interruption.
Why can we not have that in Nigeria?" João would face
his own disappointment in the ancient city. More than once
he was mistaken for her husband when she shopped for burqas,
and he had thought: *We're the real Africans. Just try mess with us!*

In her mother's room the windows were filled with the bay,
the walls were the green of a Malay shrine. He couldn't say
that to her dear mother, the super-Catholic and Galician
cook who gave them her own bed to sleep in and every day
fed them with only a pause for siesta, which João
savoured for the dreams. *What could be more perfect?* How
much lovelier could life be than here in A Coruna,
with his beloved and her mother, her sister the Sailor,
and her other sibling – devoted as a nun to children in need,
even if employed by Greek royalty, caring for their kids free
of everyday worries – and their brother the dude, the Surfer.
Don't think João couldn't see the other side: the absent father,
the young, drugged man who, one night, came up to João's beloved
and, in her ear, rambled, about remembering her, wanting her love.

"Puti clubs" the muse's mother called those places,
the small, shabby bordellos they passed on their way
to Santiago and the uncle's country house where,
again, life seemed a dream, with gardens, endless meals, Galician
spoken from childhood's inevitable depth. "Puti club," João'd said,
mimicking the good Catholic mother, thinking of the friend
of his own Mom, an Italian-Australian multimillionaire on the Way
of Santiago, still haunted, after decades, by his suicided
son, always travelling, forever restless, on pilgrimage…
I wonder if that's me, too, a hungry, wandering ghost? João
asked himself, not his beloved, who in her own exile, now
in Munich, had lived for years in London and Zurich,
surviving her own tragedy. He also wondered if he mightn't be that woman,
crazed, outside Santiago Cathedral, ceaselessly cursing the Church.

On one of those aimless, snowy afternoons
when João would have to go out or go mad, he found himself
again at the Pinakothek der Moderne, staring not into the small sketchy face
of Klee's *Angelus Novus*, once owned by Walter Benjamin,
its strange armature of being held tight by smoke and the mechanisms
of Denken. Instead, he was looking at scribbles of a moonish
grey, a small image of tumbleweed titled "The Storm",
dated 1939; when Klee, expelled from his job, was living
in the now swish Schwabing. There João once watched a film,
maybe a year or so before, on another of those days
when his dearest, the Portuguese-fluent flight-attendant, was away
in Brazil. Indeed, he'd gone, shaken, to sit in the summery park
after seeing *Malina*. That film ends with the writer in her apartment
alone, frantic, the flames erratic, leaping, blocking her way.

Göran arrived in from the Arctic cold wearing a fur hat.
They immediately went up to sit in the café
midst the cabinets of archaic figurines that
made João imagine they were in Freud's London study,
two poets as the talking-cure personified. Göran,
gentle, his speech the kind of warm quiet that seems
an uninterrupted silence, an endless, emancipated poem.
Actually, João'd imagined Göran would like this music,
like this art around them, Mediterranean, classical,
not realizing the Swede had been improv drummer, the heart
of a small jazz tribe, mathematician of the riff.
From more than a world away, having long forgotten being stiff
with Stockholm's chill, João was now more than aware
that poems are not music, only the heard, overheard: *Beware.*

Capital: a severed head, a skull. He was in the Anglophone
one, in Swedenborg House, listening to a Mexican poet,
the hall crowded and dim as the Thames city always is. Gone
from João's mind was the gloom of Blake's giants,
of epics he had read while living there pining for his lost
Galician love. The Mexican was invoking angels,
those seldom seen emissaries. João suddenly wished Buddhism
had expression without Emptiness: an unadulterated enthusiasm
for flesh, beings precise as sunlight wriggling on a roof's edge,
visitations unrecognised. One of the Mexican's angels
was a tattoo on his daughter's shoulder. Whereas, vaster
than imagined, João's guardian was that silent, refreshing wind
sweeping through the twilight's dull city, entrancing commuters
with the warm scent of incense, an intimation of more than another world.

He had planned to not write poems in Venice.
There for the Biennale and midst the sweaty tourists,
João was more lost than usual, and spontaneously would board
a vaporetto, just for the journey, the quiet boredom,
the summery rush. One afternoon, tired of the Contemporary,
he was taken to the Isola San Lazzaro, where he'd always hoped
to go, after reading that the now unpopular Lord Byron stayed
there learning Armenian, helping compile a dictionary.
Now in his room, the small library dedicated to the poet,
João fondly thought: *One of my people!* Byron's portrait
above the door looked down on donated objects:
Luso-Indian chairs, antique printed books, an Ethiopian
biblical scene happily childlike, and over an Egyptian
mummy 27 centuries old, a simple corpse, unhaunted fetish.

More than half a decade later he would again stay
in that apartment on Freundgasse, where he must say
their love began. They did first meet at a dinner in Barcelona,
and the next day he did find her reading outside La Sagrada Família.
Then, in Lisbon, kisses and bruises, and walking back at dawn…
But here in Vienna they'd had a completely orange hotel room;
their intensity had the housemaid worried, knocking at the door.
All that seems cinematic now, a forced, European dream,
a desperate hope. Instead of reminiscing, then weeping,
João envisaged this as another city, maybe equally hallucinatory,
a Bosch streetscape where he could meet Antipodean ambassadors,
wake from nightmares of packs of wild dogs and old massacres,
of trains his darling always nearly missed. The story
of their lives: her hopping aboard, declaring, "This is vertigo!"

Memories of Cape Town

Carlos, João's Brazilian uncle, poured the pasta
into a huge bowl and stirred, as if turning
a 17th Century globe. Carlos was born in Rio
and always reminded João of when as a boy he had hidden in
a cabin on a ship leaving Cape Town, almost stowed-away.
Even then João'd assumed that if he didn't get reborn in Rio de Janeiro
he would be castaway on his great-grandmothers isle,
living, pale as a ghost, exactly between Paradise and Hell.
Carlo's mother, in mourning black, silent, sallow,
awaited the supper and Tecla, her beloved, cheeky
granddaughter. And João's aunt was laughing, chatty,
clearly happy he'd returned from the Void,
not merely the urban wasteland Carlos would drive him through,
in his tour-guide mode, switching languages, showing him the world anew.

They didn't believe he could speak their Afrikaans,
so all the way to the party in Woodstock the Queen's
English was theirs, even with Sha and João's seeming
aloofness. Maybe she'd invited him along on the chance
they could kiss, start something. The hip house was red
inside, a carved wildebeest trophy up on the wall,
a guide to Xhosa on the table, everyone knowing, employed.
Sha was angelic, glorious, in her new dress, taller
than her shadow. In those days poor João's soul
was as broken as a bottle, his mind just an ear
straining to hear what shattered in the gutter. All
he thought, when Sha's gay cousin rhapsodized on the wonderful
darkness of his Congolese man, was: *We are now*
in the future we almost lost. Always innocent, our João!

Almost a nest, among the boulders up on Devil's Peak,
the rubbish, mattress of newspapers, cardboard folded
over into a bed: a bergie's home. João, weak
from a melancholy that meant he couldn't eat
and had to pretend to be present, saw that memory, unfaded,
of his last visit to the Mother City, those misty
paths along the Mountain and up Lion's Head,
where his Dad, long gone, had taken him, reminiscing
on when his own father had force-marched him, the Boy. Patriarchs
always want to be Moses, but are really disconsolate, homeless,
all wandering up the Mountain until mist or dark
descends, forcing them into caves, sleep's wilderness,
that dassies, bergies or even devils won't dare enter.
João remembers: *Men roam the world to be fatherless.*

There in the glarey Sea Point street stands his grandmother
as if in an eternally summery Lisbon, this dear, proper woman,
thin from eating too little and smoking, one eye covered
with cotton-wool, a black patch. This João remembered
nearly half a life later: their leaving and her standing alone.
She must have been talking, yet was like his own mother,
withdrawn, stoic. Still, to him she was newly from Tristan da Cunha,
love-child of a temperate nymph and privateer or sailor,
quietly hopeful of a new life after the volcano, between India
and grim London. What, João, is that your last and earliest memory,
of a castaway wordlessly blinking, looking past you,
forever staring up at Table Mountain, that huge wall, its blue?
Always remember whole continents were found by being lost.
Anyway, the Tibetans say: *Mother is space, her depths you.*

John Mateer is a poet, critic and curator. His work – published in Australia, South Africa, Indonesia, Japan, Macau, Portugal, Austria and the UK – includes art criticism, a prose travelogue on Sumatra, a novella set on the Cocos-Keeling Islands and many collections of poems. Among his collections are *Ex-White: South African Poems*, *The West: Australian Poems: 1989-2009*, *Emptiness: Asian Poems 1998-2012*, *Southern Barbarians* and *Unbelievers, or 'The Moor'* (Shearsman Books, 2013), which recently appeared in Portuguese and German-language editions. His poems have also been anthologized and translated into European and Asian languages, as well as into Farsi and Armenian.

Lightning Source UK Ltd.
Milton Keynes UK
UKHW050851290319
340121UK00001B/2/P